"I Said Mister"

ISBN # 978-1-105-55345-5

Dedicated in loving memory of Kalil McCoy...

Short Stories, Prose, and Poetry
in honor of an angel...

~ Entombed ~

[PIANO PLAYS SOFTLY]

As I sat inside myself, tears drizzling down the window pane
there was a sigh of relief hanging from the shelf in my mind
Remembering the forgotten thoughts, the buried memories
that had stayed in the lock box of my heartbeats, its walls
surrounding my pain...

Keeping it in... for all these years- the tragedy that no one knew
nothing of; the collapse of the world through our fingertips...

[Rain]

Faster, and faster the tears drizzle... spewing at my existence
oceans grow into portraits – mountains fold like an accordion
and... silence begins to invade... till it is ever still

[Quietness]

Whispers ring throughout the chromatic night, even the birds stop
everything is rolling up into a huge ball... Danseuse's cease to glide
through the thick breeze... Symphonies are not heard of through the
halls of the mind... Fire strokes through like an uncontrolled brush
and sometimes, I close the shades to my mind, searching endlessly...

[Thunder]

Rips through the core of my soul, striking everything in its path, as
rubble falls to the nakedness of my palms, and I stand in silence,
consumed by the roar of the wind... As the rain pours from the moons
architecture, closing my eyes to the p_a_i_n... a sigh of relief structures
itself around me...

[Penetrating Silence]

Devours my hungriness, arid is the thirstiness of the ground around me

(ENTOMBED CONT'D)

[Hurricane Forced Winds]

Swirling, gyrating, pouring the tears of the pain, letting it be captured taken away, burning through the breeze, the treasure of the world comes to a stop... The pain subsides, withers, dies, dissolves....
The tears begin to fade, disappear, as if they never were present... and the piano begins to play intensely...

I hung up the phone in shock... {slammed it to the floor}
my back began to slither down the plaster wall,
my mind submerged itself within {boxed in}
Tears drizzled down my flesh {sweating out the pain}
I screamed your name aloud {shaking the walls}
enclosed by the studs of my soul [trapped inside],
key-less, a window with no pane, a door with no knob... {entombed}

Thunder roared violently within {pounding me with nails}
building the walls I thought I'd never need again...
I am mummified, dry, unmoving, skin has eroded, fallen to my feet
my ivory bone is turning to dust... looking like a wood shop of another time
{saw sounds} the pain is cutting me down, devouring my soul, engulfing
my breadth... pulling the life from me, beauty is invisible... [piano plays]

It's my time...
to close my eyes, to feel the pain of everyone, and thing
It's my time...
to enclose my skies, to feel the stain of beating drums, and Spring
It's my time...
to choose my sighs, to feel the wain of feasting crumbs, the wing
as it flaps away

(Symphony plays in the distance)

Where am I, that it is dark, entombed within my own mind
watching the tears drizzle like a controlled rain, pounding, thundering through...
The breadths of time stand still...

[My soul spins around looking up]

Dancing within the atmosphere...
Calling your name still, but I hear silence, deafening, slowly killing me...

(ENTOMBED CONT'D)

[Arms drawn to chest]

Look at me...
See me witness your pain, I shout through the wind, as it is carried off
an echo is heard... bouncing from body to body... city to city... mind to mind
I say look at the beautiful sea
as it plays melancholy and lullaby's
My figure spirit falls to the dew covered ground
fist pounding wave-less...

Remember the kiss upon carmine and amethyst lips
the emotion that ran through our bodies
The motion of the ocean as we pranced though the land
of our souls, enveloping hands... ordain to follow, to lead the way
the light of the days softly, becoming the backdrop, the canvass afire
passion alas'...

NIRVANA

!!!~~~~~!!!

Your mind, the shape of an autumn vase
barnacled in yesterdays brackish tears,
a tub full of streams
its' soul,
the center of the universe,
the lobe of tomorrow
It battled- to set you loose,
to rid you of dense irons
that had oppressed you far too long...
that influenced itself
shallow within the hollows of your being,
under skies mellowed
...bewildered, not knowledgeable on what to do...
you stagger down the familiar route of tendency
fervid emotionality- erupting the world... always...
there is patience that calls... hanging its message, its mind-
to the grime, dejected and
destitute- time walks around in circles...
From the cracks in the atmosphere,
the eyes flare out from behind shadows
hiding away from the rest of civilization, its bruises,
scars lay under blankets
of phenomena, and scientific Revelations...
Satiny touches of velvet osculations...
wandering fingers, a Titan of retentions
springing from the grasp of those flirtatious doers,
the universe holding down
to the border of timepieces, and philharmonic notes;
shrieking to a halt, the metallic doorway
Days held captive in hourglasses...
rather hopeful one would assume
to fall from where you are, landing on Millay stars
and Nirvana –
... wetting all around you, on the outside of life Gorgeous...

Pearly Gates

~

High-and-dry within a blood-red sea...
my "existence" obstinate by someone, other than I
left to cognition,
with a group carrying out the death penalty with each other,
something they use to believe, now is factual...
ambivalently, imperfect, weather-beaten...rising from the
pearly gates of time... its hourglass slides, breaking
and smashing to carmine tears... its' luscious vine staggering
from its inferior, its beard tipped towards his tongue, and
to the drowsy side of life that, rubbed of its inner love...
now typeface achromatic...

Upon the blue lips of beings; cutting, drawn-out periods
of wetness, inclination, thirstiness... hurting as I close my eyes...
to the senseless slaughter of human life...
Labored to point and heart; my tears turn to liquid....
as life was pressed through and through, as tiny stems...
began with an ill health to
an activating cause, in a field of honor, that you had no cognition over...
in astonishment- you travel to the beam of light, to the vertical threshold...
walking immune, to an uncharted vista...

Cavities with no belief; individual sunken, wrinkly –
their tears adrift in an aqua-less sea... engrossing
your soul, the beloved left undelivered under models uttered...
of... an undomesticated path- to an aching, a never ending phenomenon,
its' information discriminating.... like a used machine... its moves over-flowing
with emotional triumphs... coasting closer to the point...

The worlds most ill-famed... has ordered its arms, to fall, a take over
war whirling a rebellion that would make history, educating the individual
Lucifer themselves....
Imprisoned souls... made to part their loved ones… hearts pulsating, rhythmic
values crusted to the soil, voices cut out...their breaths echo throughout the atmosphere...
I lie here... unbridled in the seashore of instance... able to count each phenomenon, that
has risen below- my body in confusion- change of state, my flesh profusely weeps,

(PEARLY GATES CONT'D)

shaking from mind to soul---
exclusive in a land shaken, defenseless by the upper hand,
unable to breath, to see a beauty once there...to concentrate...
In battle... I utter my contents... before it is too late...
focusing as I verbalize, this world
we live in, as my dreams become mislaid...
My ivory pearls to the anguished terra firma,
to the scanty caps of my knees...They have exterminated life...
even the little souls...they were the gifts of a auspicious forthcoming,
they clutched the Noesis to net income...
to come through beyond any of us...
Instead... You take everything, but I... am left to be waged
such an impact.... How do you expect me to clutch this passage....
when what I see...
makes me ill to my stomach....

When lives before me, dropped like space, consumed by your control,
power rises to frost bitten tongues....
consumed by feeling, by tragedy. Infrared are the shadows...
of forgotten dreams, its wealth unawakened in sanguinary seas-
standing in the center of a defined opening...
Assemblages lay unprovoked, in remission, or stoned by what has happened...
vector decomposition, erosion of skeletal remains...
screens the ground like debris; hidden between atmospheric beauty,
and fatigued gazes, the minutes have marked marked away, until....
there is nothing near... that once reserved itself, held by a snake pit ---
by its palms... Stripping the last bit of figure from my feature, watching
it be transferred into a departed magnetic area;
where life does not act on its own frenzy...

I returned to the shelter, a rather historic scene, and as I face through the quiet--
I begin walking continuous into the old lands to look for others...
that may be as I, and all I found were more
shades, the products of a heavenly body; just as I am now...

(PEARLY GATES CONT'D)

--- destiny covered by more departed bodies...
smothered individuals murdered for their
natural quality- Forbidden to live out their lives...
That they would soon be carried out
as a miscarriage of life by afflicting belief,
and even alteration upon a nation, that spare no likeness
to their diabolical --- The horror of blood shed,
brass instruments speak aloud, the tears
contorted into unusual shapes expectorating
to the ageless ground above...
a prediction comes forth...
as the hour sunshine gestures them by...
This ambiance I breath, its' suffocation, and state...
it is too much to absorb...

~Gushing~

Waterfalls gushing from space-less empathy
beneath orchard's consequence.
Wandering vine bandage itself around the theme, its axis
ablaze... jumping beats of a heart
descending through a summer's day, its
soul seated atop thawing ice
in a field you once dreamed...

.. .. ..Old house guitars, violins
play in understanding
over rugged shelves, where knowledge
once invigorated
ts head... its' mind stone cold, collapsing
notes, a presence
gleamed across
crashing waves, of an
abandoned ocean
. .
. . .Staring over a piano's lineament,
half-staff stars blind
the contemplations, the places
you've been, the rides through
time...fingers faster than
the speed of buoyant,
wave over the atmosphere
of once upon imaginations, and
scour the globe for bashful smiles

...Suddenly, this world...
helps itself to the dream-catchers,
events staggering
down showering mountain caps,
covered mazes
stream through excavated ditches,
once holding good times...

(GUSHING CONT'D)

.

. . .Circling back; to the smudge
we retreated from, dancing drums
dredge the days, the minutes
tick away, as tears are carried off
going back to sundowns, and morning
condensation, salt fills the air of now..

Idol of Existence

~

It's a mistral, prolonged hallucination abroad...
protruding stones- and close bones
scattered underneath unsterilized smiles...
...and unusual styles- maintenance, and breadth
shortens the irresistible finds...
under shafts, and star bursts...
resting under the conveniences of time...

Time is brief...
never should be taken for granted...
parted, circumcised...
over the articulacy of reverberating mountain
slipping old woman sea- her beauty held out---
.to the people who rest there tears on smoothing
ellipsoid of revolution ... and Brobdingnagian bowlders...
walking under the star
the helical awkwardness of unsettled thoughts...
who when not looking- seem to spasm, and set up bivouac...

Brothers and sisters... gather in an ellipse... no beginning or end...
no middle ground... no swollen, or reduced-
they shout for the exhalation- cat's-paw, ,
the chello of antediluvian seizure.... spewing of justifiable...
its perimeter turning round-a-bout, riding on Ferris wheels
and turn-tables... conjunction with life, living in time...

Are you dressed... does the influence not wet the upper lip...
Does this fewer dollars not take the mind to lesser places...
wearing your heart around those matte, bullheaded hips
on boats, and hollow vision imaginations, filling up spaces...

(IDOL OF EXISTENCE CONT'D)

Lucky... hands and adult female... horde through invisible doors
marked by existence- neighbors neither tense or suffer... avoid gaps in verse...
and they begin to drink the elbow of knee... and the music spins inside the
emptiness of absent memories- buried deeply, within crossing paths, and
tied bridges...

Stuck in the threshold of living, and the deceased... non-breathers, and ventilators
breathing out and snorting, sounding, and absent... this need to sweet talk the clapboards
forgiving these branches, have zero tune.... midnight strikes the corner stone of thunder
twice a day, and slicing the core- the stem of all mind...

Feeling nothing is not being dead- it means that the heart needs to be jump started
to feel, to see.... that this breath, shall never allow you to pass- without first permission
of the lowest idol...

...That of yourself...
of you...
beauty...
as it blows through---

Color Rain

~

I clutched open the moral door- to the upcoming adventure
to the forthcoming stories- the ones that "some" kept silent
...the untold lines...the unheard thoughts
picked them up
piled them in rows and sections, under the circumcise

Parked the frigid burning emotions- above ember coals
carefully, biological process... the faces of certainty- appeared two-fold
saw... times turn, and laggard down...
to a puddling- tears full of drained pools

Your eyes flourishing- over sunbeams-
the most delicate ribbon flew from the roots
into the most beautiful arrangement, a depiction-
shaking from its corner stone
of views, and imperial distinctions- me-lo-drama shadows
dances carefully, abroad
watching the points turn to barren spaces-
in an absence, the air dried down
on rolling hills of Paris Quintessential....

Music coiled itself into petite balls, fist size exposures-
swam from the depths of soiled colors
traveling down patterned avenues.
Contorted boulevards- dimmed in harmonica values
of satisfaction, and elastic veins arching high
over the mood-a-til- ancient counterparts come
a floor of manifestation acting upon ridiculed acquaintances

Looking through the eye socket of sorrow-
deep into the darkness, the sadness breaks away from alone
the ambushed hearts taking its own coverage,
shielded by its own dreams- hues, and oils lead me through
of shining stars and loving moments...
when the hand falls over the bones of yesteryear, till the future
one upon the other, and the look in the eyes...
you know deep down- its character rebuilds itself upon soft tint

(COLOR RAIN CONT'D)

that it has always been meant to be... this world that makes us crazy-
that tears us apart, washing through
its the dreams you color inside, its the streams of tears that wash-
that glide across my soma, my breath
away the bad, the hatred falling... the hate consumed by the light-
the birth of a million degrees burns, chars
the wave of the bursting thoughts, lines, and paragraphs...
making room for the universes to light the torch
you the only man, or lady... to gladly be... to see... this color rains

~

In My Dreams

~

Running through pieces of meadow, and rustling countryside
arms extended, I am waving, eminent through the atmosphere
...of the Worlds' most sought after emblem....

Passing Cameroonian.... hunting the heavy of era
I am coloring the breeze, to hear your voice....
Picking you up- taking a flight of stairs, through beauty
Passing airiness... towering the dark of Delaware
I am crying- taking out the fear of yesteryear....

Picking you up- musical whispers stream down from the hills...
I've seen the pandemonium of war, its looks torn to shreds
I've witnessed the everyday tears, flash in gleaming reds
I've viewed the World through superficial glasses, and time pieces

Seen wings trimmed before there start

Seen swings in the deepest ground ache
for love.... and I have closed empathy's darkness
Running through parts- of evermore ambitions, and nervous plains
as the American bison, and elephant walk proud, there horns fondly displayed

Running with beauty, in ravishing streams, laurel wreath- in invisible color...
as the chello, and the faint talk aloud, there souls astounding the ones laid
...to rest...

In my dreams; I have saw both... death and new birth

In my dreams; I have saw both... the fallen, and life
and as this vision idles down... I too taste the triggers of our World...

Whilst Butterflies Fly
~

Whilst' Butterflies dance in empathy
mocking birds gleam down on the symphony
of a dream long ago alongside the orifice
of juicy lips torturing, teasing your hide

Carving out there own itinerary
a course to love, for the decrepit above
Starving inside incertitude fury
a depiction from above, for the chalice does

I'll be that unitary;
that beats all night the illumination of a tympani
I'll be the airy; that guides the emotion, into a beautiful new morrow
I'll sandwich my arms around you,
and whisper into your heart, a beauty
that will carry you beside the ridges of yesteryear
that will carry you alongside the dedications of a single tear
and when you shout...

...I will be there to entomb your anxiety
...I will be there to rub out that teardrop
...I will be there to wipe off the calumny

Erasing your painfulness
under the running rainfall
knotting the discoloration
splitting apart the chain
that has...
held you down for so long
I will sing you a consoling song

I will be...
the bridge that keeps you together
the ridge you stand upon, as we gather
Have you forgotten
that you are a beautiful soul

Take my Breath away

~

A bead of water stirs upon wrinkly hide
in an ocean immense, filled with uncharted
a dapple of writer, sparingly utters out loud
beneath concealed desires, and rippled chaos
waves that clank, slamming me behind unto you

Soaring gulls hospitable, the shadowy masses
reach for the sunlight, lemony kisses striking inferior
unsettled with the cosmos, binding fusion, with gravity
the land and I, bathing in beauty, surrounding the moon
one with life, a purpose, determination to see it through

The ocean breeze blows on wingless beings, luscious mouths
you are my opus, the expression of surviving, being here
soothing weary souls, rocking smiles, lifting them upwards
upon my shores, the flesh of my purity, revealing kindness
they stroll along the paths of existence, wandering palms

Setting suns somersaulting over bleak, barren land
inducing tranquil sound, feeling the penetration of time
your reflection mimics the mirrors glance, the eyes of before
through contemplation, I cut deep, to the core of conduct, the
teasing of liquid, weather, and toss become my Nirvana, my resting

Closing my jewel, my eyes, meet the horizon, the fiery passion
that I may see, isn't blackened with empathy, or sized via desire
the universe as we all see it, points... stops upon fair steps, and
disclosed to me... the middle, neutral expectancy, the level to observe

Are you the murmuring inside me, swirling through each of my breaths
Far off into the distance, ravishing sea, curling butterflies beneath my flesh
someday, I'd be the bark of page, that surrounds the chapter of each saga
I am wearing my heart, outside my chest... its breathing in, and out
inhaling lives, exhaling beauty... its walking down barren sidewalks
looking for the sparkle in your azure, the gates of entry secure this thought.

:::Mama Say:::

.

I climbed that big mountain
when I got to the top, I felt like a King
looking down on the town
where I grew to be a man...
There's my mama's house on the corner
resting under the third-lamp post, mid
ways from the old school house...
...had some good times, in that school
I wonder if em' numbers I wrote on the
bathroom walls are still there...
...or the name of my first love carved in
the desk... I remember it like it was
yesterday... Mrs. Grace's class, English
I had my chair way in the back, liked
looking at everyone else...

...When she had her back to the board
I slung a balled piece of paper, like a tumbling
football, hitting Elmer smack in the head
with it... touch-down! He screamed like a pig
He knew it didn't hurt, he just wanted the
attention... I always found myself, in the old
mans office, cleaning desks in Study Hall
but I didn't fix the name in the desk...
o' no, I left it right there...

I thought of ways to get back at Elmer, for
squealing like a pig, and me getting sent to
the office all em' times... I couldn't much
figure on a suitable payback... decided to let
him be himself...Some people just cannot
help em' selves...
Gosh! That mountain made me home sick
decided to go down it, not wasting no time
I somersaulted down the front, scraped me
from head to toe, but it don't matter... it will
heal...

Got me there quicker, than driving
half-hour, hitting every red light, and going
twenty-five miles per hour, at a school crossing
Mama she passed way back when, in the house
I grew up in... nobody moved into it, they say her
spirit walks the rickety floors at night... I never
believed those tales, just fools making drama...
I'd been sitting on the old raggedy swing
and hadn't seen no sign of mama, don't know
what possessed me to half-bit believe em' fools

My eyes began to swell, like an out of control
flood, soon puddles of photo albums bed themselves
at my feet, each one making the flood rise... I walked
up the four-steps to the front porch, opened the screen
door, and stepped inside... to as if, I had never left
mama she be cooking in the kitchen, ham-hock, Lima
beans, cornbread, and a sweet smelling apple pie...
my mouth began to sprinkle hunger about the parlor
She say, "Go wash your hands, this ain't no
fancy restaurant."...
Running up the stairs, into the water-closet, running
that liquid gold, scrubbing good... mama she check your
hands before you eat at her table...Hopping on the stair-well
sliding down, just like I did that mountain...

Didn't waste no time, eating mama's cooking... she sure a good
cook, any body pass up her meals are a joker...I got up to run
back out the door... "Where you going youngster... there be dishes
to wash, gotta earn your keep, don't get nothing for free." she
said in a soft tone, shaking her head to and fro... I did the dishes
wiped the counters, swept the floor...mama said dishes, they mean
the whole kitchen, and if you going to do it right, do it all, and do
it good. That way no body can't talk bout you!..
I finished the kitchen, kissed mama on the cheek, ran back outside
to my future... sure had me a good visit with my mama...

Help Me Fly

:::

Help me!
I cannot get out
...there are no doorways
I am frightened, and missing
it is so black down here
Why do you keep me inside
I want to go outside, feel the sea
exist in the currents, the emotion
I've this tenderness that you need
to dancing, to speak aloud

The air blooms like a newborn rose
of icy forgotten arctics, a bone- coldness
that numbs me, and this huge, lilac ocean, this muscle
of an abnormal enchanted paradise, an isle you keep
enclosed around my aged, and somersaulting mind
stimulating conversations with just these walls
pregnant thoughts waiting to burst from this room
virginity setting up camp, under the veins of light
bars stripping me, imprisonment within freedom...

Chocking on yesterdays empathy, old graffiti on the
lineage, capillary walls of this recessed space, cushion
desires florid from lack of effect, or motive
How am I too... continue on, to swim in the felicity
of salty, candied tears...Am I to be locked away in this
abyss, this well of fear, of letting me go, of seeing me fly

I'd like to tell you... I would stay with you evermore
sinking my roots deep, underneath your feet, and playing house
but I can't... cos' there is so much for me do, faces to contact
tears to wash away, hurting to rub out, people to unify... under this
union called life---

(Cont'd)

Death doesn't make me different, I am the identical person, that I always have been... When you wave your hand in front of you, this is me, I am blowing you kisses...When you feel chills run up your spine, that is me, wrapping my wings around you... When life feels heavy, I will be there to remind you, everything will be okay...
Please let me go!
So that I too can... feel the beauty around you
So that I too can... feel the innocence of the wind blowing through
Please let me out! In order for me to continue to exist, you must ....release me from your heart

MOSES

Beneath the orchestra of snapping chordophone strings
and jubilant cases of misused, unwanted fiddle tools
lives a powerful sacred being...
Never looking behind at the structured figures of absent bones
and ignored tartan and tattered trousers, or of his abused
ophidian skinned...boots, worn as a good luck spell...

Outside his spirit, love crowds in all directions, kicking and
pulsating... as he purges through vapor-less elevation get-a-
ways...and logging roads closed down...

He never thought of himself...
always favoring the people, the souls exhumed under the soil
the lives fallen, down the burrows core, and the immaculate
deities, his yellowish finger nails... showed of illness
An illness,he never spoke much of..for he was too busy
saving those who needed to go on, those who had a future
his name was Moses, and he hungered for continuation

At first light, when the shades drew up, exposing the virginity
of dawns early grace, he packed his mind inside his soul
and strolled down memory lane, looking back, to the survivors

Rose
!!!

I am laying on a plot of Caucasian roses
staring far into the acclivity charcoal-gray
While my mind roams the star scheme
exploring the aphotic pits of philosophical theory
....It is so beautiful, come look for yourselves...
To the right is Blue blood Point, and over there...
...that's Sovereigns Embankment, and above us... it's Unity

My sky-blue eyes... are bound by its virgin beauty
I never want to leave this secret plain, I'd stay here for infinity
so, that this feeling- never___leaves___me...
this emotion never strays.... never suffers....
I am laying on a bed of blonde roses
absorbing life through my pores, my vena the train
taking the beauty to points, it has never been
and as I lay here searching for further existence
breathing you in, caging it into tiny crevices
I remember... that the universe is large, but
so are we... that no matter the understanding or the
versification, the cognition or imagery... there'll always
be my patch of opalescent roses...

Time is so vicarious sometimes; it flows without help
swimming underneath the princess sea, it drowns, and
it fights... fighting for love, reaching for its own Nirvana
, the benignant
that lasts for a life time...

Like a youngster, it spills over itself, and it falls in wells made
of effectual liquid, but it gets back up
and continues to go, the strings of a horologe dancing...
its performances showering down, leaving breaths of time

(Cont'd)

The empathy surpasses all expectancy, it drives itself
through opaque waters, through wetlands of destiny, and rests
its chin on life...
There is a plane of content in everything we touch
a expectation that keeps us upright through each perturbation
A fire that burns,,,, and eyes that see nothing else...
but the most ravishing sunsets, and the cottony clouds
the swords of the sun, as they point towards the Universe
Where signaling whisperings declare there itinerary, its distinction
that detaches it from all beginnings... and as it flies, envelopes of roses
breathe in the World, and disperses it out... around themselves...

"A Man and His Instrument"

::::::::

:::::::

::::::

:::

:

I came from the old schoolhouse
things weren't handed to you
on a silvery platter.
That it was a sin to move in
sympathies stone pool
that you had to make it beautiful
or all your dreams would burst.

I knew what sweat and blisters were
worked two jobs; to support my sick mama
and my own dreams.
I hit bumps, and windy curves
fought with some big Lama's (beasts)
Heard laughter twist to screams.

One day...
When I turn's sixteen
I decided to go after my dream
not let nothing get in my way
I bid them great day...
went to the musical store, got me
a fifteen-dollar instrument
taught myself how to play
and earned me an honest pay.
Got my first gig in a tiny bar
off the Interstate...

I showed them white folk a thing
played Jazz, like that's all I ever knew
the whole place was clapping,

(Cont'd)

I was a star
I found my true destiny, my fate
and I ride like a shooting spring star
just like mama; when she flew to be an angel
I was the musical ace happening
I didn't get no fancy help, or key to no gate
You know them white folk
sat there and clapped at me

They did comment to me though
Say... We the fool, cos' you go and prove us wrong.
I guess I did...
cos' I became something,
the white folk
told me I couldn't.

Today,
Ima' an old black folk -
playing jazz
to the white folk....

Noesis

<>

On a road far from you, I stand, unitary, solo
scouring the barren-less land with the sapphire
verity of the matter, we make our own courses
A stage of copiousness circles us, flipping liquid for spines
strung out on language, feeling the mind inside you
an explosion of cognition, showering downward

Knowing all this time, people have crossed this very fork
beginning, to end, the end... pages, and titles sprouted
the azure making room for the bloody sweat, and the
rumors, o' how they fly to out-of-town places, vapor alarms
sounding off, the helical effect starts, and everything
comes blooming down, down on the arctic, cold ground

Noesis has cast a pathology; it has challenged you
upside over the unification collisions, and the tango divides
hides a Amerind file announcing a concealed possession, a symbol
awaits the influential, a bona fide sentiment poses within

We wonder if the wind; had not pushed our backs
where would we be today, would we be in the spot where we
first began... no wings, or legs to maneuver our orifices, our own
egos... they'd be drifting motionless over waterless ocean tides

The years have gained ground, hung around to watch us age
an aspiration; when we were younger, to grow up... to age gracefully
moving step upon step under the solar of knowledge, the walls
of our mind uncircumcised under twin moons; arches bouncing
above our heads, somersaulting through paper thin lives

(Cont'd)

The fears manifesting, and coiled over greenery, carefully, placed on a vagrants log, stripped of certainty- a commitment balanced by an inner desire, a fiery passion ablaze inside our souls, a core of existence pledged to never give up, to pull the anchors, and to swim across the great straights, to reside within virgin flesh riding high on the wind, skipping over mountains tongues, against all odds we are the few, who've made it through...

Welcome to life... and all that it has offered the individual

If I Die

.

If I die
before I have the chance to love
Don't ask why
just watch the wings fly above
Paint me across the sky
and catch the stars as they unfold
letters tucked next to your heart
Fill the rainbow with the eye
of enchanted dreams... as they are told
listen carefully, these words of a song

If I die
before I have the chance to love
Don't cry
just watch the swings soar above
Love is in the air... and it missed me
all those stares... blank, and an empty sea
dropping coins in a ravishing fountain
each time I etched your name in a mountain

If I die
don't cry, or ask why
just walk with my heart, and see me fly above
This love... I leave for you
high above... as the wind blows through
you will see me...

Pieces of a Soul

–.--

Pieces of a soul
lay scattered on an empty beach
her waves shattered, and eyes closed
peeking from behind her lash sheers
every once in awhile...

Her brown fur brows tacked down by sea shells
as time trickles out to sea, one by one...
and her heart it begins to beat hard, upon
rock drums, and elephant flesh... whaling at
every breadth, that she pulls from deep within...
...she is unable to speak, no utterance escapes
her chapped, crimson lips....

...Her azure eyes freckled, and burning from the
salt water bath, enthralls, thrusts outward shouting...
a quaint glistening peers from behind her iris, signaling
a fond farewell... to sea she takes her first step...
after a short time, she plunges under...

Swimming deep into the abyss of heaven...
she witnesses beauty in all mediums, its background
melting before her now salt eyes, shaking from the spine
she purges further down into the deep blue, ...
she is never seen again....

The Call of Thunder

-

Under the mantle of nighttime
'neath the sentiment of illumination
I feel your breadth, drop-off, within
the trauma of vena, the release of liquid
slowly, silently flowing, down into the ravine
of yore, and I empty ever so slightly
falling into another period

Thunder began to rake through the season
'neath the relics of bountiful memory
the figure skins one artifact at a time
under the brilliance of bounding bolts of energy
perhaps, the dear will stay
and everything would be the aforesaid
free as an raptor, tearful onward
the soma, of contagion, the end of fiery calamity
slowly, silently flowing down into the alteration
the intravenous spinning of content, looms of phantasy
pour nightly, calling from the hormone
yearning for yet, the appearance of one's gone
and one's yet fitted...

Palace Tears

~

Must time discontinue
to surcease an epoch
of Romanticism, and
solitariness...
has no humanity
perceived the expression
in a silenced fleur-de-lis
or the ascent of the educatee...

Why is there but, driblet to tumble
beyond purview, and Au naturel lunation
thus, we all attempt to be a speaker
of efflorescence soul, its commencement
And... as it centers itself, upon signaling prima
a tiny ontogeny emerges from the aphotic sea
presenting the creation of life below
colored super-cilium, and poverty-stricken fingers

His visage remains interred under battle ruins
and mud artifacts, his quality compromised
by the touch of hand, and the whisper of breadth
He is viewed merely, a adult male, with no asperity,
nor a watercraft with no vanes, as the sapphire's
hunger begins to diminish, above the Indian file, the
palace in the beauteous cobalt, where emotion is now...

A King With A Queen By His Side

<>

Empathy plays no boundaries, as it swings from soul, to ravishing dream
Let me touch you, just one time... I want to feel your heartbeat, as it flies
There is no greater joy, than to see an individuals smile, upon glazed face

Swirling in its' own breadth, recounting its own steps; one by one
continuing on; over mountains, through oceans... beneath the boiling sun
Bare to the world, the words slither, like a spigot it drips onto one another

Far away, across the oceans, the door to beauty opened up, and grew
casting brightness abound, the swords of stricken bay, and when it did
beautiful rose gardens bloomed, covering the hate of hell, and the liquid

I saw your spirit come out of the caves, you've been exploring the writings
focusing on the core, its rectifying existence; when time met the calm soil
knowing the artifacts, and documents of space-less uniqueness's...

You fell... the chello's of life's joys played no music, nor silence
the window to eternity disappeared in shadows- growing each slender hour
and the roars of hungry mountain lions brought you to tired knees, cowering

Once I saw your reality, I was moved by glittery wing, and beak
the pages turn with ease, as I read the story chapter by chapter, and my
heart comes alive- spilling to my lap, and like a puddle it grew

Empathy is "love me for me-and never look back.", cos' it will never change
except the things you cannot change, and change the things that you can
Carry on with a smile, and walk like a King- with a Queen by your side

A Man & His Boo

[I ask that you read this carefully, there is a lesson to this...]
-

He has his boo in his mouth, all day long...
makes me feel like, there is no place I belong...
maybe one day, he will notice me, wanna be
with me...

---She has this boo in her mind, playing along
want me to put my dream down, lay it to rest
close the lid to my hopes, and desires...

He thinks I don't see, how he looks at his boo
disrobing the metallic flesh, to the bare bones
or, how is heart begins to thump, when its here
staring him in the face...

--- She is backing up, if she think I'm gonna give
it up, I ain't no fool from some city town, or no
beggar looking for a hand out....

He don't get it, momma said he be like this
she said, the man got it bad for his boo, I need to
step down, let him have his own space with his
boo...

--- Don't she see; me and my boo, we got it going on
gonna shake up the town, rock the roofs off buildings
make a name for ourselves- just me and my boo...
I don't need this crap from her-

(Cont'd)

***He so fine, shake em hips like there ain't no tomorrow
play his boo with everything he got, rattle those cages
he have to lay her down sometime, and when he do, I
gonna run after that thing...***

***--- I ain't never seen a woman...
jealous over a harmonica, but a man cannot have more
than one boo....***

Urban Dreams by a Father

<><><>

I came home
pa he in the parlor
watching The Jefferson's
he said go in the kitchen
got something for you

I walked in the kitchen
smelt' ham-hocks, and cabbage
cooking, pa he cooks sometimes
when he know I work hard

On the table, two packages lay quietly
they were calling my name, open me
wrapped in yesterdays news, top articles
Carefully, I removed the clothes-line rope
used as a ribbon, and bow...
The big box, it had a fancy dress, and shoes
a pretty hat, and stockings, a purse to boot

I didn't understand... didn't I make a good
daughter, clean, and cook for my pa, Why is
he sending me away... Wasn't I good...
I ran into the parlor, said pa... why...
he told me open the small package, then ask why
I tore into that small box, and found a Greyhound
ticket, one way, to my dreams...
Why pa......
am I not a good daughter...
I take care of you good...
Why you want to send me away....
You my baby girl...
but, the Lord he calling me child
Can't keep the Lord waiting...

(Cont'd)

But pa...
I don't want to go...
Not ready for you to leave...
I love you pa...

Baby girl...
he calling me, its my time, I gotta go
your dreams, they calling you...
its time for us both... to go-

I don't like this pa...

Baby girl.... its not for you to understand
for the reasons are not clear...
one day...
when you have babies
you will do the same thing...

For now...
chase your dreams
encase your soul with love
finish what I began
make me proud...

My pa... he know best~

An angel in God's paradise
leaves behind family & friends
<>
Kalil Ree'na Paris Israel McCoy
20 years old
A graduate of Andrew Jackson Senior High School
Class of 2o11
She danced with the Tiger Sensations

We hold a distinction
somersaulting tears trickle down
forming oceans of love

Existence
barrels through the wind
breadths of belief

We live by his hand
therefore, we must thank him
bind your hearts and souls

Praise his existence, distinction, and love

Every Night

<><>

My mind tears of a beautiful waterfall,
on a hill top in the middle of nowhere
Every day is a conflict to stay afloat,
in a raging sea of motion-less waves
...turning the pages of a book I cannot hold tight to my chest...
I shutter its contents;
watching the fiery flames beat down around me...

And as I stand here,
watching the globe spin out of control, my heart grows
to free itself from this bond, this relationship with life,
which somersaults me through
...mornings peek in on the virginity of dawn's face,
trying to make heads or tails of this act
eyes baring the existence of negativity,
as people bounce around trying to find fault...

I am falling across the empty space, of a star filled sky,
grayish-black consumes its eyes
composing the architecture of a still afternoon,
time capsules transport me to the other side
...pouring contents from a ruptured soul,
pain devours the happiness of my skeletal remains
skies awakened, but soon falling back to sleep,
beneath carpeted bridges...

PHILHARMONICS

Ambrosia lines the paseo to the soul, acquitted years ago
moments in time, that touched down-
landing all its contents in a convenient package, called life
...heartbeats racing through the speedway of your heart,
embracing for the finish line...

Each second ticks away; germinating around the arena of the cosmos
intensity grows, deepens with each nectar word said, to rise and fall
between the disrobing breadths of time... When the clock strings
begin to snap, and all is still...

Sipping on the characters of fine wines, and violin philharmonics
eternity sometimes tends to slip through your fingertips, slithering
through the breeze of today's emotion... Moments to cradle inside
the souls of ancient lore, and modern day scrolls...

I remain settled, sun-swayed by hatred.... the skin naked, spreading
over my palms... Eyes bestowal its nestled tongue, the displayed patron
...its earth swallows, and maintains, shedding the sadness, the weak,
and isolated tears... scooping love all around...

Broken Faces, Soldiers

~

He sat on the corner of life;
barely, holding onto the strings that supported the axis,
of the beautiful universe.
Dehydrated, he collapsed on a barren-less plain,
and his mind submerged itself in salty sea tears...
defining his unending struggle...to stay afloat.
His palms ached of ink, describing his life- before, he was homeless.

I, an existence, once ruled the world of me!
I served my country, protected the people...
in return they stare through my flesh,
my bones eroded over the mountainous caverns.
Where humankind swelled,
hard times caught them by the neck.
True breeders of this planet,
always thankful for what was allowed to them.
I, the existence, also am...thankful, but my fellow man,
sees not the breadth of my tongue,
this soul has traveled many roads, hung onto the taste –
that dwell on my capillaries. That looks pass my ugliness.
You see I did not come back the man I was.
War does that to you; you go in fighting,
and come back fighting yourself. I do not understand why...
but they think we are crazy, our minds stayed over there...
Flashbacks drive us to the dark side of society,
where hiding from the general population,
is more satisfying than facing the faces who look down on us.

My best friend from the war,
he couldn't handle society, after twenty-years of fighting the enemy.
He couldn't stand himself, the things he had to do,
because his orders said so. He came home with all of us...
but never woke the following morning.
He shot himself with his own gun, mind matter painted over his walls.
I cried silent tears that day...

(Cont'd)

You learn to do that as a soldier, to not throw-up your feelings.
Got to be a man; inside and out!
People call it a weakness, we call it pride.
I am not the only one that is out here, there are many more,
I lost track of the total. The streets are a war zone within there selves.
Never a dull moment out here, always some kind of foolishness going on.

Yesterday, I picked up cans, took them to the recycling plant...
I got five-dollars for a days work.
Sounds like slave wages to me, but I really can't complain.
No one wants to hire a broken man, that has angel wings sewn to his back.
Not to mention, being soft spoken, and singing within the wind...
Sweet Home America... Times are difficult for everyone, yet...
few show it- its called ego.
The person sitting across from you hasn't any money or coins in his pocket.
While the man sitting in a three-piece suit,
sipping on white wine, has no sense in his pockets.
These are the people who kill me... looking at me all strange.
Once, I was so hungry, I saw me a three-piece stick walking down the Boulevard,
tipping his hand at all the beautiful ladies.
I stopped him, and asked if I could work for a meal,
and he brushed me off, walking away with a smile.
I guess it is back to picking up cans,
I can always go to a fast food joint, and get me the dollar menu...
My belly won't talk to me then!

www.ingramcontent.com/pod-product-compliance
Ingram Content Group UK Ltd.
Pitfield, Milton Keynes, MK11 3LW, UK
UKHW051134260726
13967UKWH00010B/3038

9 781105 553455